# Jeffrey Dahmer

# Milwaukee

# Monster

## The Shocking True Story of Serial Killer Jeffrey Dahmer

Roger Harrington

# Table of Contents

# Introduction

Known as the Milwaukee Monster and the Milwaukee Cannibal, Jeffrey Dahmer was one of the most well-known and prolific serial killers in history. Dahmer terrorized the Wisconsin city for thirteen years murdering seventeen known victims from 1978 until his capture in 1991.

The name Jeffrey Dahmer is synonymous with the phrase serial killer and stands out due to his victim profile, M.O., and the excessively violent and bloody nature of his crimes. The homosexual Dahmer was different in the sense that all of his victims were men compared to the vast majority of male serial killers who tend to be heterosexual with female victims.

Dahmer is also different in the sense that he showed some remorse for his crimes after his apprehension as well as realized what he'd done was wrong. Still, Jeffrey Dahmer is considered a real-life boogey man; a monster with the labels or rapist, cannibal, murderer, and necrophilia.

Over twenty years after his own murder in prison, the grisly story of Dahmer still equally fascinates and sickens those brave enough to look inside.

# Early Life

Jeffrey Lionel Dahmer was born on May 21, 1960, in the city he would later terrorize, Milwaukee, Wisconsin. He was the oldest son of Joyce Flint Dahmer and Lionel Dahmer. Joyce worked as a teletype machine instructor and Lionel was a student at Marquette University where he was working towards a degree in chemistry.

Dahmer as doted on as a toddler and had a relatively happy childhood for the most part which is just one of the many things that sets him apart from many other serial killers. His childhood did however share one prevalent characteristic of serial killers; a domineering mother.

Joyce Dahmer was known to friends and neighbors to be argumentative and constantly demanding attention. Lionel Dahmer's university studies and job kept him busy and was away from the family home often. This left Jeffrey alone with Joyce, who didn't spend much time with him when Lionel was around as she demanded as much attention as possible from him.

Joyce also suffered from anxiety due to constantly demanding attention and trying to appease her husband. The couple often fought in front of their children. When Jeffrey was still very young, Joyce Dahmer attempted suicide by overdosing on Equanil, a tranquilizer drug. As Jeffrey grew older, Joyce spent much of her time in bed recovering from what was reported as her "weakness and illness", which was most likely anxiety and/or depression. Joyce later developed cerebral palsy.

Jeffrey was later described as an "energetic and happy child" despite his parent's marital issues. This all changed when Jefferey underwent surgery for a double hernia when she was almost four years old. After the surgery, his personality changed and he was noticeably calmer and timider.

On his first-grade report card, a teacher wrote that Jeffrey was "a reversed child whom she sensed felt neglected due to his mother's illness." His peers also later described him as quiet and withdrawn but he did have a small group of friends throughout his life.

As a child, Dahmer developed an interest in various animals. While this looked harmless as a child, this hobby would later evolve into something much more sinister. His friends stated that Dahmer collected large insects, dragonflies, and butterflies which he would place in jars.

When he got older, Dahmer and his friends would collect animal carcasses from the roadside and the woods behind his family's home. One of his friends later stated that Dahmer would dismember the animals and store various parts in jars in his family's toolshed. In a sick Frankenstein-like experiment, Dahmer would also experiment with the dismembered parts and see if the different animals would fit together. It is also believed that on one occasion, Dahmer impaled the head of a dog on a stake behind his house.

This odd fascination with death, dismemberment, and control was the first sign of Dahmer's dark future. When he was only four years old, his father recalled that he was transfixed when he had to remove a dead animal from underneath the family home. Lionel Dahmer said that his son was "oddly thrilled" by the sounds the bones made when they clinked together.

Shortly after his incident is when Dahmer's fascination with bones and animals emerged. Along with collecting bones and various insects and animals, he would also explore and examine the bodies of live animals.

In October 1966, the Dahmer family relocated to Doylestown, Ohio after Lionel obtained a job as an analytical chemist in the nearby city of Akron, Ohio. Two months later, the Dahmer's youngest son, David was born. Joyce had let Jefferey pick out the name of his little brother.

Two years later, the family moved again. This time to the town of Bath, Ohio. When Dahmer was about eight years old, he asked his father during a family dinner of chicken what would happen if he placed the chicken bones in bleach.

His son's interest in science, especially the chemistry aspect of his morbid questions delighted Lionel who had previous concerns about Jeffrey's lack of social skills and general laziness. He then showed his son how to preserve bones, something which he would later use in his murders.

As Dahmer grew older and into high school, he became more socially withdrawn. Former classmates later reported that he was an "outcast." They also recalled that he would wear an army fatigue jacket to school and smuggle in both beer and wine which he would drink during school.

HIs drinking started around age 14 and wasn't limited to school hours. A classmate later recalled an incident when he saw Dahmer drinking from a bottle of gin during a class. When he asked him why he was drinking in the middle of school, he said Dahmer replied, "it's my medicine."

During his high school career, Dahmer had average grades. His teachers noticed his strong apathy and that he was, for the most part, an underachiever. He did briefly join the high school band and showed some talent as a tennis player. Teachers and classmates described him as being very polite and intelligent.

Even though Dahmer was considered an outcast by his peers, he could also be friendly and outgoing. He was known to play pranks and his friends and classmates, although these pranks could have been ill-advised and were most likely a cry for attention.

As his high school career went on, Dahmer's grades continued to fall and his alcohol abuse increased. He also became more withdrawn socially. His parents hired a tutor for help with his education which did little to further Dahmer academically.

It was during high school that Dahmer discovered his homosexuality but did not tell his parents until he was much older. He later recalled that he did have one homosexual relationship as a young teenager but never had sexual intercourse with the boy.

As Dahmer grew more comfortable in his own sexuality, his dark, twisted sexual fantasies began to emerge. He later that he started to fantasize about having complete control over a submission partner and that the thoughts grew into an obsession.

This dominant and submissive relationship became a lifelong fetish for Dahmer and eventually crossed with more violent thoughts including dissection and later murder.

Along with a dominant and submissive relationship, Dahmer also developed a rape fantasy about a certain male jogger who he saw on a regular basis. He later admitted that this sexual fantasy is what led him to also fantasize about having sexual intercourse with unconscious bodies which was later a major aspect of his murders.

Dahmer attempted to make his fantasy a reality. One day, he hid in the bushes on the jogger's daily route with the intent to attack the jogger with a baseball bat. Luckily, the jogger did not pass him that day. Dahmer never tried to attack the jogger again. He later said that the incident was the first time he ever attempted to attack another person.

During his senior year of high school, a teacher spotted Dahmer drinking beer in the school parking lot. The teacher questioned him about it and Dahmer told him he was having troubles at home and that he'd told the school's guidance counselor. This was not true. Lionel and Joyce Dahmer had been fighting more frequently and in front of their sons which was clearly taking a toll on them.

Several months before Dahmer graduated high school, his martens divorced after attending couples therapy as an attempt to save their marriage.

1978 was a vital year in Dahmer's life. Not only was it the year he graduated high school and the year his parents divorced; it was the year he committed his first murder and unleashed the monster that would later terrorize Milwaukee.

# The First Murder

While most new high school graduates are preparing to attend college or enter the workforce, Jeffrey Dahmer was ready to commit his first murder.

The time for Dahmer was perfect. He was eighteen and living alone at his mother's house as she and his younger brother, David had recently moved to Chippewa Falls, Wisconsin. Lionel Dahmer was also living nearby in a motel.

On June 18, 1978, Dahmer picked up an eighteen-year-old hitchhiker named Steven Mark Hicks. Dahmer lured Hicks into his car with the promise of taking him back to his house to drink alcohol. Hicks, who had been hitchhiking to a concert took Dahmer up on his offer.

Once back at Dahmer's house, the two young men drank and listened to music together for several hours. When Hicks attempted to leave, Dahmer bludgeoned him to death with a ten-pound dumbbell.

Dahmer later said, that Hicks, "wanted to leave but I didn't want him to." He hit Hicks twice from behind while he was sitting in a chair. Once he was unconscious, Dahmer strangled him to death. He then ripped the clothes off of his body and stood and masturbated over the corpse.

The next day, Dahmer dismembered and dissected Hicks's body and hide it in the crawl space of his house He later moved the body to a shallow grave in his backyard. Several weeks after burying the body, Dahmer dug up the corpse and pared the skin from the bones.

He then dissolved the flesh in acid, flushed it down the toilet, and crushed up the bones with a sledgehammer and scattered them in the patch of woods behind his house.

Six weeks after Hicks's murder, Lionel and his new fiancée stopped by the Dahmer home to find Jeffrey living there alone. In August 1978, Dahmer enrolled at Ohio State University as a business major.

Much like high school, his short time in college was not a success. Still abusing alcohol on a regular basis, Dahmer spent most of his one semester in college drinking and rarely attending classes.

He did not pass a single class. His father came to visit him once and found his dorm room full of empty liquor bottles. Lionel had also repaid for his son's second semester at college in the hopes that he would stay enrolled and continue his education.

Dahmer left Ohio State after only three months and returned home to Milwaukee. Lionel was extremely upset and disappointed in his oldest son as he had attended college and greatly valued education.

Lionel still upset with his son for dropping out of college, urged him to join the Army. Dahmer joined the United States Army in January 1979. He was trained as a medical specialist and was eventually transferred to Baumholder, West Germany where he served as a combat medic.

His military records showed that he was an "average or slightly above average solider." Dahmer's military career was short-lived. He was honorably discharged in March 1981 after being declared unsuitable for service due to his decreased performance from his still heavy alcohol abuse.

In 2010, almost twenty years after his death, two soldiers came forward with allegations that they had been raped by Dahmer on multiple occasions while stationed in West Germany.

After being discharged, Dahmer was debriefed by the military and given a plane ticket to go anywhere in the United States. Instead of returning home to Wisconsin, he went to Miami, Florida. Dahmer later said he went to Miami because he didn't want to face his father after being discharged and that he was "tired of the cold."

Once in Florida, he started working at a deli and rented a room in a motel nearby. He continued drinking heavily and was soon unable to pay his motel bills which led to him being evicted for nonpayment.

For several months after he was evicted, Dahmer kept his job and lived on the beach. Later that year in September, he called his father, who was now living in Ohio and asked if he could live with him for a while.

Lionel accepted and allowed his son to live with him and his new wife who required him to complete a majority of the housework in exchange for room and board while he looked for work.

The change of scenery did nothing to curb Dahmer's drinking. After being in Ohio for only two weeks, he was arrested for drunk and disorderly conduct for which he was fined $60.

After his arrest, Lionel attempted to unsuccessfully wean him off alcohol. In December 1981, after only living with his father and stepmother for three months, Dahmer was sent to live with his paternal grandmother in West Allis, Wisconsin hoping that her influence would lead him to stop drinking and obtain gainful employment.

Dahmer held much affection for his grandmother and for a short time was on his best behavior. He would take his grandmother to church, willingly partake in household chores, and followed the rules she had set in place for him.

While he still continued to drink, the time he spent with his grandmother inspired Dahmer to turn his life around. He trained and worked as a phlebotomist at the Milwaukee Blood Plasma Center for almost a year before he was laid off.

Soon before Dahmer lost his job, he was arrested for indecent exposure on August 7, 1982, after exposing himself to a crowd of 25 women and children at the Wisconsin State Fair. He was convicted and fined $50.

After his arrest and job loss, he was unemployed for two years and lived on money given to him by his grandmother. In 1985, Dahmer found another job as a mixer at the Milwaukee Ambrosia Chocolate Factory where he worked until he was apprehended for the murders.

Dahmer worked at the factory from 11:00 p.m. until 7:00 a.m. six days a week with every Saturday night off. Those working hours would later become an ideal schedule for Dahmer to carry out his infamous murders.

An incident occurred after Dahmer started working at the chocolate factory which again jumpstarted his fetish for a dominant and submissive relationship. One afternoon, Dahmer was sexually propositioned by another man while at the West Allis Public Library.

Dahmer later said that he did not take the man up on his offer but that the sexual nature of the situation was the beginning of his fetishes which soon evolved to murder.

He soon started visiting Milwaukee's various gay bars, gay bookstores, and bathhouses as a way to satisfy his ever-growing sexual urges and needs. At one point, he even stole a male mannequin from a department store that he kept in his closet and used for sexual simulation.

His grandmother found the mannequin one day and ordered him to throw it out. This incident was the first in a long line which would eventually lead to his grandmother forcing him to move out.

With his new job and Saturday night off, Dahmer found himself with a stable income and a place to live which gave him more freedom than ever before. He used that freedom explore his sexuality and further continue his ever-present alcohol abuse.

Dahmer becomes a regular fixture at local gay bars and bathhouses which are saunas or steamboat facilities with numerous rooms that are used for men to engage in homosexual intercourse. He later referred to as his "relaxing places." At these bars and bathhouses, Dahmer picked up numerous sexual partners. This seemingly never-ending parade of conquests brought out Dahmer's psychopathic impulses more than anything ever had before.

He later said after his arrest for the murders that "I trained myself to view people as objects of pleasure instead of people." His natural psychopathic nature, his intense drive for sexual pleasure, and his fantasies of having a dominant and submissive sexual relationship were all catalysts in Dahmer's escalation into madness and murder.

Dahmer later said that in June 1986, he started to drug his sexual partners with sleeping pills and/or feeding them liquor laced with sedatives before raping their unconscious bodies.

Word soon spread among the gay bars and bathhouses that Dahmer was drugging and raping men. His actions got his bathhouse membership revoked.

Upset with no longer having access to one of his "relaxing places", Dahmer's desires festered and grew into something much more sinister. He said that soon after he was banned from his former bathhouse that he considered stealing the corpse of a recently deceased eighteen-year-old male for sexual reasons after seeing his obituary in the local newspaper.

According to Dahmer in his later interviews, he said that he went to the gravesite and attempted to dig the coffin up but found the soil too hard and left. While this incident is no doubt disturbing, it is only a fraction of the horrific things to come.

# The Milwaukee Cannibal Strikes Again and Again

Dahmer's serial killing spree truly took off nine years after he'd killed his first victim. Before he became known as the Milwaukee Cannibal, Dahmer was arrested one more in August 1986 after he was caught masturbating in public in front of two twelve-year-old boys near the Kinnickinnic River in Wisconsin.

At first, Dahmer admitted what he'd done but then changed his story saying he was urinating in the woods unaware there were two juvenile witnesses present. His lawyer was able to get the charge altered for disorderly conduct. Dahmer was sentenced to one year of probation and court-ordered counseling.

The urge to kill hit Dahmer again in November 1987. One night, Dahmer met twenty-five-year-old Steven Tuomi at a bar. He then took him back to his hotel room at Milwaukee's Ambassador Hotel where he'd rented a room for the night. It was not unusual for Dahmer to rent a hotel room for a night out on the town as at the time he was still living with his grandmother.

Once Dahmer had Tuomi back at his hotel room, he went back to his old trick of giving his conquest a cocktail of liquor and sedatives. Dahmer later recalled that he had no intention of murdering Tuomi but had only intended to date rape him.

After a night of heavy drinking and raping Tuomi, Dahmer said he woke up the next morning and found Tuomi lying underneath him on the bed dead. He later said that Tumor's chest was crushed and covered in bruises along with having blood seeping from his mouth. Dahmer said that his own fists and forearms were bruised as well.

Dahmer said that he had no memory of committing the murder and claimed that he did not set out to murder Tuomi, something that he reiterated several times during his later confessions. He said that he "could not believe this happened."

Considering the horrifically violent murders in his near future and admitting to them, Dahmer not remembering doing something that he felt compelled to do is very hard to believe. However, considering his excessive and extreme alcohol abuse he could have been telling the truth.

If what Dahmer said about not remembering killing Tuomi was true, then alcohol lowered Dahmer's inhibitions and he acted out his murderous fantasy without remembering it later. This is plausible considering Dahmer's history with alcohol.

Even though Dahmer said he had no memory of committing his second murder, he later claimed responsibility for it. At the time of Tuomi's murder, Dahmer was still living with his grandmother which would soon prove difficult to carry out his murderous agenda even though he had a bedroom in the basement with a door to the outside.

To transport the body back to his grandmother's house, Dahmer purchased a large suitcase which he placed the body in and hid in his room. A week later, he then severed off the arms, legs, and head from the torso, removed the flesh from the body and cut it into small pieces.

This was followed by him placing the flesh into plastic bags, wrapping the bones up in a sheet, and smashing them into pieces with a sledgehammer like he'd done with his first murder almost ten years previously.

He kept the head for a total of two weeks before disposing of all of Tuomi's remains in the trash. He did keep the severed head for two weeks which he'd soaked in an industrial-strength detergent called Soilex which he took from the chocolate factory.

After the detergent soaked and removed the flesh from the skull, Dahmer then bleached the skull and used it during masturbation. The bleach eventually dissolved the skull and

Dahmer also smashed it up with a sledgehammer. Dahmer said that the entire process of the desecrating Tuomi's corpse took two hours.

Tuomi's murder set off Dahmer's urge to kill and in the weeks after he started to seek out his next victim which soon became plural. Dahmer used the local gay bars as his hunting grounds where he would find young men, usually younger than him or close to his own age.

Dahmer would then take them back to his grandmother's house where he would be drugged via sleeping pill or by another powerful sedative prior to sexual activity. He kept this method up for some time and it sadly proved to be successful again and again.

The need and urge to kill struck Dahmer again two months after Tuomi's murder. Even though

Dahmer said he didn't remember killing his second victim, this needs to kill had to have been aggravated by something in his life. Or he wanted to be able to experience taking the life of another human being and actually remember it.

His third victim was a fourteen-year-old Native American male sex worker named James Doxator, who Dahmer killed on January 16, 1988. The two met near a gay bar in Milwaukee and offered him $50 to come to his apartment with him to take nude photos. This was a tactic Dahmer used on several of his victims.

Dahmer took Doxator back to his grandmother's house. The two engaged in sexual intercourse then Dahmer strangled him to death on the floor. He hid Doxator's body in a basement closet for a week before dismembering it. He also removed the flesh with acid, again smashed the bones up with a sledgehammer and kept the skull.

Dahmer also used boiled and bleached Doxator's skull and used it as a masturbation tool like he had with Tuomi's. He also put Doxator's flesh and smashed bone fragments in the trash. Another two months passed before Dahmer struck again. Two months seemed to be Dahmer's standard serial killer "cooling off period" which is the time between each murder where the killer will relive, replay, and fantasize about their last kill until the memory wears off and they must kill again and repeat the cycle.

Dahmer's disgusting cycle was due again on March 24, 1988. This time the victim was a twenty-two-year-old bisexual man named Richard Guerrero. Like this other victims,

Dahmer and Guerrero met outside of a Milwaukee gay bar called The Phoenix.

Dahmer again lured the man to his grandmother's house. This time it wasn't for nude photos, Dahmer simply offered him $50 to spend the night with him. Guerrero accepted the stranger's invitation.

As Dahmer's murders escalated, so did the violence and sexual perversion involved in them. The murder of Richard Guerrero was the beginning of that. Dahmer offered Guerrero a drink laced with sleeping pills. Once he was passed out, Dahmer strangled him with a leather strap. Dahmer then performed oral sex on Guerrero's corpse.

This escalation of violence and necrophilia in the murders was perfectly summed up by the killer himself. Dahmer said in an interview with

Inside Edition, "It's a process, it doesn't happen overnight when you depersonalize another person and view them as just an object. An object for pleasure and not a living breathing human being. It seems to make it easier to do things you shouldn't do."

Along with several other quotes from Dahmer, this shows that he was aware of this escalation as well as that he knew what he was doing was wrong but his violent and sexually demented impulses and desires counteracted what little sound judgment he had.

With Guerrero, Dahmer dismembered the corpse within twenty-four hours after the murder. He also continued with the removing of and dissolving of the flesh in acid as well as bleaching the skull and using it for sexual stimulation.

As with his similar victims, Dahmer kept Guerrero's skull for some time before smashing it and throwing it away in the garbage several months later.

Almost exactly a month later, Dahmer planned to murder another young man. This short amount of time between the Guerrero murder and this potential victim was shorter than the time between the previous murders.

This could be for a number of reasons. Mainly, that Dahmer had become addicted to killing and his cooling off period had grown shorter because of his need and addiction. It could also indicate that he was not satisfied with his previous kill.

The true reason will never be known but whatever that reason inadvertently saved the life of a young man. On the night of April 23,

1988, Dahmer lured another young man back to his grandmother's home. Like those who were murdered before, the man was given a cup of coffee laced with sedatives.

Soon after he started drinking what was meant to be his last cup of joe, Dahmer's grandmother called downstairs asking, "Is that you, Jeff?" This prompted Dahmer to reply in such a way that indicated it was, in fact, him and that he was alone and not planning on unknowingly murdering another victim in her basement.

Fearing that somehow his grandmother sensed what was about to happen, Dahmer decided not to kill this man. Instead, he let him finish the cup of laced coffee until he became unconscious. Dahmer then took him to the emergency room at a hospital in Milwaukee.

This instance was one of the times Dahmer's humanity shown through the psychopathy. Dahmer is one of the rare serial killers who appeared to show some remorse for what he'd done. Although his show of remorse was slim and possibly not genuine, Dahmer realized that the things he'd done were wrong.

In several interviews which are available to view online, Dahmer said several things that if taken out of context would appear to have been said by a completely different person and not a deranged serial murderer.

He said, "It is hard for me to believe a human being could have done what I've done." Dahmer also said that he didn't actually enjoy the act of killing these seventeen men. This is extremely hard to believe and frankly ridiculous considering everything Dahmer did to these men.

Dahmer indicated that the killing "was the least satisfactory part" and that his entire serial killing career was based on the concept of control.

In 1994, three years after his apprehension Dahmer gave a now-famous interview with reporter Stone Phillips for Dateline NBC. This particular interview is one of the essential pieces of evidence inside the mind of a serial killer as well as a prominent source for all things Dahmer considering the story is coming from the man himself.

In the interview, Dahmer said that "No, the killing was not the objective. I just wanted to have the person under my complete control, not having to consider their wishes, being able to keep them there as long as I wanted."

If what he is saying was the truth then Dahmer is significantly different than the vast majority of serial killers and should be put into a category all his own. With most serial killers, the primary objective is to kill for whatever reason.

Whether that reason is a sexual thrill, mission-driven, or for power and domination, the primary goal for these killers is to simply kill. With Dahmer, it seems that killing was what he had to do to get to his primary goal of having a completely submissive (most likely sexually submissive) person and that the primary goal itself was not to kill.

Dahmer did not kill again until almost a year after his previous victim. This year-long break from killing seemed to be as a result of outside factors and had nothing to do with a cooling off period.

In September 1988, Dahmer's grandmother grew concerned about his behavior and finally after several years confronted him about it. She complained about him bringing numerous men back to the house late at night as well as complained about foul smells coming from his basement room.

His grandmother spoke to Dahmer's father (her son) about the men and the smells. One day, Lionel Dahmer visited the house and inspected Jeffrey's room. When he found a black, sticky substance which he, as a chemist knew to be the byproduct of acid on living tissue, he assumed Jeffrey had been experimenting with animals like he'd done when he was younger. Lionel didn't question it any further.

This resulted in his grandmother throwing him out of her house. Dahmer found an apartment located at 808 North 24th Street in Milwaukee which he moved into on September 25, 1989. The next day, he was arrested for drugging and sexually molesting a thirteen-year-old boy. Dahmer had lured the boy back to his new apartment under the pretense of getting paid to take and pose for nude photos.

It is unclear if Dahmer intended to murder the young teen. Based on his previous crimes, it was very likely. Dahmer was convicted of enticing a child for immoral purposes and second-degree assault in January 1989. His sentencing was suspended until May of that year after serving only one week in jail.

On May 23, 1989, Dahmer was finally sentenced to five years probation, sent to live in a halfway house for a year with work release privileges under the condition that he keep his job at the chocolate factory. He also had to register as a sex offender in the state of Wisconsin. At the sentencing, Dahmer stated the obvious, "I am an alcoholic and a homosexual with sexual problems."

In the time between his arrest and sentencing, Dahmer found time to add another victim to his list. On March 25, 1989, Dahmer met an aspiring model named Anthony Sears. Sears was twenty-four-year-old, mixed race, and someone that Dahmer later said he found "exceptionally attractive."

Dahmer later said that on the night of March 25, he had not planned to commit another murder but rather when the opportunity presented itself, he did not turn it down.

It was Sears who approached Dahmer that night at a local gay bar named La Cage. The two men went back to Dahmer's grandmother's house which he'd moved back into after his arrest. It was there that Dahmer repeated the same murderous song and dance of his previous victims.

However, this one was slightly different as it was the first one of his victims that Dahmer stored the body parts of in acetone. This is due to the fact that Dahmer found him so attractive.

Once Sears was back at Mrs. Dahmer's house, the two men performed oral sex on one another before Dahmer drugged him with a laced drink and strangled him.

The next morning while his grandmother was out running errands, Dahmer drug the body upstairs where he decapitated it and flayed the flesh from the corpse. He threw the flesh away in the trash along with the smashed up bones.

Dahmer then sliced off Sears's head and genitalia and stored them both in a jar full of acetone. In a very risky move, Dahmer kept the jars hidden in his work locker until he moved to an address which would soon become infamous in Milwaukee and American true crime history.

After completing his time in the halfway house on the work release program, Dahmer was paroled two months before his scheduled release date. He then stayed at his grandmother's for several months until he moved into the apartment which would later become a macabre museum of murder.

On May 14, 1990, Dahmer moved out of his grandmother's house for the last time and into the last address he would ever have that wasn't in a federal prison. Apartment 213 located on 924 North 25th Street in Milwaukee is where Dahmer would commit some of his even more heinous crimes and where he would soon get caught.

The apartment was in a high-crime, majorly African- American, blue collar neighborhood and was a striking difference from the houses he grew up and his grandmother's house where he'd been for the past several years.

However, the rent was cheap (only $300 a month) and provided Dahmer with the opportunity to live in a place where he could easily blend in with the other crimes being committed all around and not be bothered.

Once Dahmer moved into his apartment, he removed the jars of acetone containing Anthony Sears's head and genitals from his work locker to his new home. At some point, Dahmer had painted the genitals.

Within several weeks of moving and settling into his new apartment, Dahmer added his sixth victim to his ever-growing list. This time, the victim was 32-year-old Raymond Smith.

Dahmer again lured Smith back to his apartment under the impression he was going to get paid $50 for sex. Once the two men arrived at apartment 213, Dahmer started his murder ritual all over again, giving Smith a laced drink and then strangling him to death.

The next morning, Dahmer added a new step to his process. He took his newly purchased Polaroid camera, posed Smith's body in several sexually suggestive poses, and took multiple photos. The photos were a key piece of evidence in Dahmer's trial.

After the morbid photo shoot, Dahmer dismembered Smith's corpse in his bathtub. He then boiled Smith's arms, legs, and pelvis in a large steel kettle with the Soilex detergent. This caused the flesh to be easier to remove from the bones.

Before he placed the dismembered body in the detergent solution, Dahmer said that he had sexual intercourse with Raymond Smith's corpse. He said that this was the first time he'd engaged in sexual intercourse with the full corpse and not just parts like he had with the skulls of several of his victims in the past.

Dahmer then took his process one step further and dissolved the rest of Smith's bones, minus the skull in acid. He took the skull, spray-painted it and placed it on a shelf next to the skull of Anthony Sears.

Only one week passed before the urge to kill as a means to control struck Dahmer again. Like the incident several years previously in his grandmother's basement, this murder did not go as planned and ended up in Dahmer himself becoming the victim instead of the other way around.

On the night of May 27, 1990, Dahmer invited another young man back to his apartment. On this particular night, when Dahmer was preparing his token drug-laced cocktail to give to his victim, he accidentally got the glasses messed up and drank the laced drink himself.

The following morning, Dahmer woke up and found that the young man had stolen his watch, $300 cash, and several items of his clothing. Dahmer never reported the incident to the police as he obviously did not want to invite them into an on-going crime scene. Even though he never told the police, he did tell his probation officer he had been robbed.

A month later in June 1990, Dahmer killed again without accidentally drugging himself. This time, the victim was an acquaintance of Dahmer's, twenty-seven-year-old Edward Smith. This was the first and only time that Dahmer was known to have murdered someone he knew. This is a risky move for active serial killers and an almost guaranteed way to get caught, or at least get noticed by the police.

That night, Dahmer drugged and strangled Edward Smith after the two men performed oral sex on one another. For this murder, Dahmer decided to dismember the corpse and store it in the freezer for several months in the hopes that the body would retain it's moisture as overtime Dahmer had discovered that immediately placing the bones and flesh in acid and then bleaching the bones would cause the bones, primarily the skull which was clearly Dahmer's favorite part to turn brittle and crack.

After a few months of being in the freezer, the corpse of Edward Smith did not retain any moisture. Dahmer placed the skull in the oven in the hopes that the heat would dry it out and he would be able to add it to his collection.

This plan backfired and the skull exploded in the oven. During Dahmer's lengthy confession about a year later, he told police that he felt "rotten" about Edward Smith's murder because he destroyed his body and wasn't able to keep any part of him.

Dahmer's excessive need to keep the classic serial killer trophies from his victims was tied back to his need for control. He believed that if he could keep a part of someone, that he would have better control over them. Dahmer himself even said, "The only motive that there ever was was to completely control a person; a person I found physically attractive. And keep them with me as long as possible, even if it meant just keeping a part of them."

While this does tie into Dahmer's desire to completely control another human being, the keeping of the skulls and other various body parts was also a way for Dahmer to relive the crimes by viewing his trophies, which is a common aspect of serial killings.

Dahmer's next kill happened about three months later on September 1, 1990. Twenty-two-year-old Chicago native Ernest Miller met the man who would soon take his life on the corner of North 27th street in Milwaukee where he was spending the Labor Day holiday weekend.

Dahmer took Miller back to his apartment where Dahmer attempted to give him oral sex. Miller told Dahmer, "that will cost you extra."

Dahmer then gave Miller a drink laced with sleeping pills. This time, Dahmer only had two pills, a standard dose and was not enough to render the man unconscious. This prompted Dahmer to change up his M.O.

When Miller started to grow sleepy, Dahmer slit his throat, hitting the carotid artery using the same sharp, hunting knife he used to dismember bodies. This caused Miller to bleed to death in a manner of minutes. Dahmer then took the body to his bathtub where he used to murder weapon to dismember the body.

Dahmer later told police during his confession that while he was dismembering the body, he kissed Miller's lips and talked to his severed head. He then took Miller's, biceps, heart, and other mounds of flesh, wrapped them in plastic bags and placed them in the freezer.

He then boiled the remaining flesh with Soilex, which he said turned the human flesh and organs into a "jelly-like substance. After this was complete, he removed the flesh from the bones, placed it in the trash, and this time decided to keep the entire skeleton which he'd soaked in bleach for a week prior and then left to dry on a towel.

Miller's severed head was also kept in the freezer for some time before Dahmer decided to boil it to remove the flesh and brain. The skull was then painted and coated with an enamel protectant and kept next to his other skulls.

Only three weeks later, Dahmer committed his next murder. On September 24, 1990, Dahmer met a twenty-two-year-old father named David Thomas at the Grand Avenue Mall. The two men flirted and Dahmer convinced Thomas to go to his apartment with him for drinks as well as take photographs which Dahmer said he'd pay him $50 for.

Thomas agreed and Dahmer drugged him. However, once he was drugged, Dahmer stated that he no longer felt attracted to Thomas. He stated that he was afraid that when Thomas woke up he would be rightfully angry that he'd been drugged.

Instead of face that, Dahmer decided the best plan was to strangle and dismember the body. Sine this was not someone he found attractive and/or wanted to control, Dahmer disposed of all of Thomas's body parts. He did take photos of Thomas's corpse in sexually suggestive and grotesque poses like he had with several other victims previously. These photographs were later used to identify Thomas's body.

After the murder of David Thomas, Dahmer did not kill again for five months, which was the second longest cooling off period during

Dahmer's active killing years beside the nine-year gap between his first and second murder.

From October 1990 until February 1991, when his next murder took place, Dahmer later told police that he tried to lure men back to his apartment in order to kill them but was unsuccessful every time. His probation officer, who he was still required to visit for his sex offense several years earlier, and Dahmer himself later said that during this time, he was experiencing increased feelings of anxiety and depression.

Dahmer said these feelings manifested from his sexuality, his solitary lifestyle of working night shift and being an introvert and psychopath, as well as some financial troubles brought on by his pervasive alcohol abuse and frequent barhopping. He also said around this time, he started having suicidal thoughts.

In February 1991, Dahmer started killing again in what would the start of his last murder streak. His next victim was seventeen-year-old Curtis Straughter. Dahmer said he spotted Straughter at a bus stop by Marquette University.

He was able to easily lure the young, broke college student back to his apartment with the promise of money in exchange for posing for nude photos as well as sexual intercourse. Straughter eagerly accepted the offer and went back to Dahmer's apartment with him.

Once back at his apartment, Dahmer drugged Straughter and strangled him with a leather strap like he'd done to so many other young men before him.

Dahmer then dismembered his body. He kept Straughter's skull, hands, and genitals. During the process of dismembering Straughter's body, Dahmer took photographs of the process which he kept in his apartment. Dahmer also kept Straughter's hands and genitals.

On April 7, Dahmer's next victim suffered an infamous fate which was later known to be synonymous with Jeffrey Dahmer. That day, Dahmer ran into nineteen-year-old Errol Lindsey while Lindsey was on his way to a hardware store to get a copy of a key made.

Even though Lindsey was supposedly heterosexual, Dahmer was able to get him to come back to his apartment with the promise of money for posing for photos. Lindsey, who Dahmer said was broke at the time accepted the offer.

Once at Dahmer's apartment, he drugged Lindsey with sleeping pills. When Lindsey was asleep, Dahmer conducted one of his most cruel and horrifying experiments.

Making sure Lindsey was asleep, Dahmer grabbed a power drill and drilled a small hole into the front of Lindsey's skull. He then poured hydrochloric acid into the hole and subsequently into Lindsay's brain.

Dahmer did this as a way to put Lindsay into a permanent submissive, zombie-like state. Dahmer said on numerous occasions that his was his primary goal for his killing spree.

Dahmer said that shortly after he poured the acid into Lindsey's skull that he woke up and said, "I have a headache. What time is it?"

As this was not the result Dahmer intended, he drugged him again with more sleeping pills and strangled him. He then decapitated the body and flayed Lindsey's skin. Dahmer kept the skull after boiling it to remove the flesh and brain.

With this murder, Dahmer decided to further experiment with the flayed skin. He placed it in a mixture of cold water and salt hoping to permanently preserve it. This did not work as the salt corroded the flesh. Dahmer later said he was upset that this and the acid in the brain did not work.

Shortly after Lindsey's murder, the residents of the Oxford Apartment Building where Dahmer lived started to complain of foul odors coming from his apartment. Residents also reported occasionally hearing the sound of a chainsaw coming from Dahmer's unit.

The then-manager of the Oxford Apartments, Sopa Princewell contacted Dahmer on several occasions to address the issue. Dahmer told Princewell that the smell was from his freezer breaking down, which he said caused the contents to spoil. The second time he was contacted about the smell, Dahmer said that it was from some tropical fish he owned that he just died. It was confirmed that Dahmer did, in fact, own a tropical fish aquarium so this excuse was not far-fetched.

Dahmer's next victim was a thirty-one-year-old man named Tony Hughes, who Dahmer killed on May 24, 1991. Dahmer again offered Hughes $50 to go to his apartment to take nude photographs. As Hughes was deaf, he and

Dahmer communicated with one another with handwritten notes.

Hughes was then drugged and strangled. Dahmer then dismembered his body three days after the murder. He took more photographs of the corpse in various stages of the dismemberment process. Dahmer boiled his head and kept the skull.

Only two days later, Dahmer struck again. As with most serial killers, his kills drastically increased in both volume and violence. On May 26, 1991, Dahmer ran into fourteen-year-old Konerak Sinthasomphone, who was the younger brother of the boy he'd molested in 1988.

Dahmer offered Sinthasomphone money to pose for photographs. Sinthasomphone, supposedly knew who Dahmer was and hesitated on the offer. He eventually reluctantly agreed.

Once at Dahmer's apartment, Sinthasomphone took off his clothes and posed for photographs wearing only his underwear. Dahmer then drugged the young boy with a drink laced with sleeping pills.

When Sinthasomphone was unconscious, Dahmer performed oral sex on him before attempting to create another submissive zombie to cater to his every perverted whim.

Dahmer then drilled a hole in Sinthasomphone's head and poured the hydrochloric acid in through the frontal lobe. Dahmer said he took Sinthasomphone's body into his bedroom where the body was Tony Hughes was still intact. He said that he believed

Sinthasomphone saw Hughes's body but was too afraid to say anything about it.

Sinthasomphone becomes unconscious again. While he was passed out, Dahmer laid by his body and drank several beers. He soon left to go to a nearby liquor store and have another drink at a bar on the way.

The next day in the early morning, Dahmer returned home to find Sinthasomphone sitting naked on the corner of the street near his apartment building. Sinthasomphone was talking to three women in Laotian who were hysterical as he'd described what Dahmer had done to him.

Dahmer approached Sinthasomphone and the women and explained that the two were lovers and that he was drunk and confused. The women told Dahmer they had called the police to come investigate.

When the police arrived, Dahmer told officers John Balcerzak and Joseph Gabrish that Sinthasomphone was his nineteen-year-old lover and that he was drunk and acted out on a regular basis when he was intoxicated.

The women told the police officers that Sinthasomphone had told them that he was experiencing anal bleeding from being raped by the man standing next to them. The officers told the women to mind their own business, to not interfere with the incident as it was a "domestic dispute."

The officers covered up Sinthasomphone with a towel and walked with him into Dahmer's apartment. Dahmer continued to reiterate that they were lovers. The officers did not notice any evidence of the numerous murders that had taken place there but did make note of the strange odors in the apartment.

Dahmer even said that the officers did not inspect his apartment very well and that he was sure he was going to get caught then and there. The officers believed Dahmer and left Sinthasomphone with him. Officer Balcerzak was fried for allowing the young boy to stay with the sex offender and serial killer. He later contested his firing and was reinstated as a Milwaukee police officer.

Dahmer said that the officers told him to "take good care of Sinthasomphone" and left. After the police left his apartment, Dahmer said that he gave Sinthasomphone another frontal lobe injection of hydrochloric acid. This injection proved to be fatal.

The next day, Dahmer took the day off work in order to dismember both the bodies or Sinthasomphone and Hughes. He later pointed out that Hughes's body was in his bedroom when the police stopped by. After dismembering both of his most recent victims, Dahmer kept both of their skulls.

On June 30, Dahmer traveled to Chicago for the annual gay pride parade. There he met twenty-year-old Matt Turner at a bus station. Dahmer told Turner he was a professional photographer and asked him if he could photograph him.

Turner accepted and went back to Dahmer's apartment via Greyhound Bus where he was then drugged, strangled, and dismembered. Turner's head and internal organs were placed in plastic bags and then put in the freezer.

Five days alter for the July 4th holiday, Dahmer went back to Chicago presumably impressed with the ease of finding and luring victims back to his apartment, which was 90 miles away.

Back in Chicago, Dahmer met twenty-three-year-old Jeremiah Weinburger who he convinced to come back to Milwaukee with him and spend the weekend. Dahmer drugged Weinburger, drilled a hole in his skull, and injected boiling water into the hole.

Much like the hydrochloric acid, the boiling water did not work the way he'd hoped. Weinburger fell into a coma soon after the water and sleeping pills combined in his body. He died at Dahmer's apartment two days later.

Two weeks later on July 15, Dahmer met twenty-four-year-old Oliver Lacy several blocks away from his apartment. Lacy then agreed to go back to Dahmer's apartment to pose for nude photographs. The two men had sexual intercourse prior to Dahmer drugging Lacy.

Dahmer later said that he liked Lacy and wanted to prolong the amount of time he spent with him while he was alive. Dahmer then decided to drug him with chloroform. He then strangled Lacy while he was under the influence of the chloroform.

Dahmer said he had sex with Lacy's corpse before dismembering it. He said he put Lacy's heart and head in the refrigerator and his dismembered skeleton in the freezer.

Again Dahmer called into work for the purpose of dismembering a body. His request was granted but he was suspended from the factory when he called into work sick the next day. Four days later, he was fired.

Upon hearing he was fired, Dahmer took out his frustrations on yet another victim. This time it was twenty-five-year-old Joseph Bradehoft, who was also strangled. He left Bradehoft's body in his bed for two days covered with a sheet. Bradehoft, a father of three from Minnesota was in Milwaukee looking for work to relocate with his family.

Dahmer later said when he removed the sheet, he found the body covered in maggots. He then decapitated Bradehoft and s kept his head in the freezer. Little did Dahmer know, Bradehoft would be his last victim.

# Apprehension

Several weeks after what was to be his last murder, Dahmer set out to add another victim to the list. He found three men and offered them $100 to come to his apartment and pose for nude photos, drink beer, and keep one another company.

Only one of the three men, thirty-two-year-old Tracy Edwards agreed to accompany Dahmer back to his apartment. Edwards later recalled that he immediately noticed a foul odor in the apartment and noticed boxes of hydrochloric acid on the floor.

Edwards and Dahmer talked for a few minutes. Dahmer asked Edwards to look at his tropical fish. When Edwards turned his head, Dahmer tried to place a pair of handcuffs on Edwards but he was able to get away.

Dahmer then had Edwards follow him into his bedroom. Edwards later recalled that Dahmer had numerous posters of nude men on his wall and that a videotape of The Exorcist III was playing in the room. He also noted a large, plastic 57-gallon drum in the corner of the room the contained a foul-smelling odor.

Edwards said that Dahmer held out a knife and said that he was going to take nude photos of him. Edwards said he obliged and started to unbutton his shirt to appease Dahmer and said he would take the photos only if Dahmer would remove the handcuffs.

Dahmer ignores him and turned towards the television. Edwards then said Dahmer started rocking back and forth and chanting. He then turned to Edwards, placed his head on his chest, and told Edwards he was going to eat his heart.

Edwards said he kept telling Dahmer they were friends in an effort to avoid getting attacked or killed. He even said that he considered jumping out of the apartment building windows if he could get away rather than be killed by Dahmer.

Edwards then suggested they go into the living room where there was air conditioning and grab a beer from the kitchen. Dahmer agreed. When the men made it into the living room, Edwards waited for Dahmer to look away for a bit.

When that happened, Edwards told Dahmer he needed the use the bathroom. Instead of going to the bathroom, Edwards stood up from the living room couch and punched Dahmer in the face.

The blow knocked him down and gave Edwards enough time to run out of the front door. Several minutes later, Edwards flagged down two police officers on the corner of North 25th Street, the same street where Dahmer lived.

Edwards told the officers that "a freak" had handcuffed him and tried to kill him. He then asked the officers to use their handcuff keys to remove the ones on Edwards's wrists. Both officers tried but neither one of their keys worked.

Edwards then led them to Dahmer's apartment and told them everything that happened. When the police officers and Edwards arrived at Dahmer's apartment, he let them in and said that he'd placed the handcuffs on Edwards but did not say why he'd done so.

After Dahmer failed to provide a reason for the handcuffs, Edwards then spoke up and said that Dahmer had held a knife to his chest while they were in the bedroom. Again, Dahmer ignored the remark and offered to go get the handcuff keys from his bedroom.

The officers beat Dahmer to his own room and prohibited him from entering while they were in here. Officer Mueller, who was present at the scene noticed the large knife Edwards had described. Upon looking further in the bedroom, he noticed an open dresser drawer where he sat some of Dahmer's Polaroid photos of decomposing bodies.

Officer Mueller approached his partner, Officer Rauth and showed him the photos he said, "these are for real." When Dahmer noticed the officers with is photos, he tried to fight them.

The officers were able to easily overpower him and had him handcuffed and arrested in no time. Back up was called and soon more police arrived at the scene. When Dahmer was handcuffed he said to the officers, "For what I did I should be dead."

Officer Mueller said while they were waiting for the backup to arrive, he found the various body parts in Dahmer's fridge, including a freshly severed head on the bottom shelf.

When more police arrived to search the apartment of horrors, they were shocked at what they found. The following was found in apartment 213: a total of seven skulls, a plate of blood drippings in the refrigerator, tow human hearts, a portion of arm muscle wrapped in a plastic bag, a bag of various organs in the freezer, human flesh stuck to ice that was in a bag in the freezer, two complete skeletons, a pair of hands, two severed penises, a mummified scalp, and the 57 gallon drum full of acid.

Police also found a total of 74 Polaroid photographs of various bodies posed and dismembered. The Milwaukee Medical Examiner later said of the apartment, "It was more like dismantling someone's museum than an actual crime scene."

Once Dahmer was arrested and taken to the local police station, he immediately started confessing to his crimes. Over a total of two weeks, Detective Patrick Murphy and Detective Patrick Kennedy questioned Dahmer for over sixty hours.

During the confessions and interrogations, Dahmer waived his right to an attorney and said he wanted to confess to everything, saying that he "created this horror and it only makes sense I do everything to put an end it to."

He then told the detectives every single detail of all of his crimes, including all seventeen murders, including his first one in Ohio in 1978. He admitted to engaging in necrophilia and having sexual intercourse with and using the viscera and other body parts of victims for sexual stimulation. He also confessed to cannibalizing the bodies of his victims on multiple occasions.

Dahmer went into graphic details on how he'd killed various victims and the processes he went through to dismember their bodies and storing their bones and organs. He confessed to having kept the skulls of some of his victims in the hopes that he might one day build a shrine to them. He said that the altar was for his own personal meditation.

Dahmer also provided police with the names of several of his victims.

On July 25, 1991, Dahmer was charged with four counts of murder. Less than a month later, that number than gone up to eleven. Once he confessed to the murder of Steven Hicks in Ohio and bone fragments matching Hicks were found where Dahmer said he buried the body, he was also charged for murder in Ohio.

Dahmer was not charged for Steven Tuomi's murder as there was no evidence linking him to the crime and he still maintained that he didn't remember committing the murder. He also wasn't charge for the attempted murder of Tracy Edwards.

At his preliminary hearing on January 13, 1992, Dahmer pled guilty but insane to a total of fifteen counts of murder.

His trial began on January 30, 1992. Almost instantly when the story about the Milwaukee Cannibal broke, the news media sensationalized the story which led to it being the story it is today.

During the trial, one of the main arguments was Dahmer's mental state. Clearly, a person who had committed such horrible acts was insane. However, options differed.

The defense argued that Dahmer was, in fact, insane and that he was completely driven by his paraphilia for necrophilia and his urges to kill and that his sexual issues and his urges to kill rendered him unable to control his actions.

An expert witness for the defense, a forensic psychiatrist diagnosed Dahmer with borderline personality disorder, schizotypal personality disorder, necrophilia, alcohol dependence, and a psychotic disorder. These multiple diagnoses of mental disorders was a plot by the defense to make Dahmer appear so mentally unstable that he could not control his impulses to kill.

Many of the witnesses in the trial were expert witness mental health professionals as there were no witnesses to the crimes other than Tracy Edwards. These individuals offered various insights into Dahmer's psyche and mental state.

Prior to the increase in murders and before he was fired from his factory job, Dahmer appeared to lead a normal, stable life. This is a clear sign of an organized killer which Dahmer was for some time. However, the short time frame between his last murders proves that Dahmer was clearly losing his footing and started to mentally break down.

The prosecution rejected these claims of insanity stating that Dahmer was aware of his actions the entire time he was killing and that he deliberately took measures to ensure he was not caught and that there was no evidence linking him to the crimes, which was true for several of his victims as Dahmer had disposed of the bodies so well that no traces of them were ever found.

Another forensic psychiatrist, Dr. Phillip Resnick who testified for the prosecution did not agree with the defense's argument that

Dahmer was insane. Resnick disagreed with the diagnoses that Dahmer suffered from necrophilia because he preferred his sexual partners alive based on the fact that he used the acid and boiling water to create his perfect submissive partner who would be alive and not dead.

Another psychiatrist, Dr. Fred Fosdel testified that he believed Dahmer to be of sound mind when he committed his murders and that he did not suffer from any sort of mental disorder.

Dr. Fosdel said that Dahmer was a "calculating and cunning individual, able to differentiate between right and wrong, with the ability to control his actions."

Fosdel also agreed that Dahmer did suffer from a necrophile paraphilia but that he was not a sadist. Another forensic psychiatrist, Park Dietz for the prosecution agreed that Dahmer was not suffering from a mental illness because he purposefully planned the murders and made sure there were no witnesses, which worked.

Dr. Dietz claimed that his planning and execution of the murders did not make them impulsive acts. Also, the fact that Dahmer purposefully did not murder several of his intended victims (such as the young man who was in his grandmother's basement the night she called down to them) shows that he did have some control over his actions.

Dietz also made an interesting connection between Dahmer's murders and his alcohol abuse. Dahmer himself even said that killing was not his favorite part and that he mainly killed as a way to control the person and get to their "insides."

Dietz correlated that Dahmer had to drink in order to kill. He said, "If he had a compulsion to kill, he would not have to drink alcohol. He had to drink alcohol to overcome his inhibition, to do the crime which he would rather not do."

His conclusion is accurate based on Dahmer's own claims about the murders. Dietz also noted that Dahmer was known to identify with a sympathize with the villain characters in Return of the Jedi and The Exorcist III.

With this theory about the fictional characters, Dietz mentioned the fact that Dahmer would often watch scenes from these films before going out to the bars to find a victim. Dietz's diagnoses of Dahmer included substance abuse disorder with a focus on alcohol, paraphilia, and schizotypal personality disorder.

A court-appointed psychiatrist George Palermo brought a different and the most accurate approach and diagnoses to Dahmer and his crimes. Palermo said that Dahmer's murders were a result of "pent-up aggression within himself. He killed those men because he wanted to kill the source of his homosexual attraction to them. In killing them, he killed what he hated in himself."

Palermo stated that Dahmer was a sexual sadist based on his murders and what'd he'd done to the bodies of his victims. Palermo also diagnosed Dahmer with antisocial personality disorder but declared him legally sane.

Another court-appointed mental health professional, clinical psychologist, Dr. Samuel Friedman theorized that Dahmer's longing for companionship is what drove him to kill in order to create his submissive person to cater to his every need.

Friedman testified at Mr. Dahmer's trial and said, "Mr. Dahmer is not psychotic." He spoke kindly of Dahmer, describing him as "Amiable, pleasant to be with, courteous, with a sense of humor, conventionally handsome, and charming in manner. He was, and still is, a bright young man."

Dr. Friedman diagnosed Dahmer with a personality disorder not otherwise specified, obsessive-compulsive disorder, and that he possessed sadistic traits.

The trial which was highly publicized by the media due to the graphically violent nature of the crimes, only lasted two weeks. On February 15, 1992, Dahmer was ruled to be sane and found not to be suffering from any mental disorders at the time of the murders.

The fact that Dahmer was not declared insane was a shock to many, perhaps even to Dahmer himself. Fellow serial killer John Wayne Gacy even commented on the matter in an interview in 1992 shortly after Dahmer's sentencing. Gacy said, "I don't know the man personally, but I'll tell ya this, that's a good example as to why insanity doesn't belong in the courtroom. Because if Jeffrey Dahmer doesn't meet the requirements for insanity, then I'd hate like hell to run into the guy that does."

Dahmer was sentenced to life in prison plus 10 years for two of the murders with the remaining 13 counts of murder carrying a mandatory life sentence plus 70 years per Wisconsin law. The death penalty was not an option in this case as Wisconsin had abolished capital punishment in 1853.

Three months after his sentencing and verdict in Wisconsin, Dahmer was extradited to Ohio where he was tried for the 1978 murder of Steven Hicks. In a court hearing that lasted a meager 45 minutes, the jury found Dahmer guilty and was sentenced to another life sentence on May 1, 1992.

Once Dahmer was sentenced and transferred to prison, his troubles did not stop and once in prison, Dahmer got a dramatic exit.

# Life and Death in Prison

After Dahmer's sentencing, he was transferred to the Columbia Correctional Institute in Portage, Wisconsin. During the first year of his sentence, Dahmer was kept in solitary confinement for his own protection as he was a very high profile inmate due to the media attention his trial and crimes received.

When his year in solitary was completed, Dahmer himself consented to be moved to the general population but his security was still heavily monitored. He was assigned work detail which he spent daily in a two-hour block of cleaning the prison toilets.

While in prison, Dahmer requested that Detective Patrick Murphy, one of the detectives Dahmer confessed to after his arrest send him a copy of the Bible. Detective Murphy agreed and Dahmer became interested in Christianity and converted to the religion soon after.

This is a common tactic for incarcerated criminals, especially those who feel some sense of guilt or remorse towards their crimes like Dahmer did. His father, Lionel Dahmer was also a born-again Christian and encouraged his son's new-found interested in the religion.

Lionel provided him with many Christian books including several books on creationism. In May 1994, Dahmer was baptized by, Roy Ratliff a minister in the Church of Christ who had come to visit him in prison. After he baptized Dahmer, Ratliff would regularly visit him in prison and the two men become friends. Ratliff also led the weekly prison chapel service.

Dahmer took Ratliff's teachings to heart as well as the principles of his new faith. Dahmer told Ratliff that he felt he was sinning against God by continuing to live because of all the horrible things he'd done to others.

In prison, Dahmer mainly kept to himself and was a model inmate. In July 1994, another inmate named Osvaldo Durruthy attempted to kill Dahmer by slashing his throat with a razor blade embedded in a toothbrush. Durruthy attacked Dahmer as he was returning to his cell from the prison chapel.

Dahmer received several wounds from the attack but was not seriously injured. He did little to fight back. Dahmer's family said several times that he was ready to die and accepted the punishment he knew he was going to receive in prison.

Dahmer also retained a good relationship with his parents and stepmother while he was in prison with both sets of parents calling him a weekly basis. Although Dahmer and his mother were not close, (at that point they hadn't seen one another since Christmas 1983), the two rekindled their relationship while Dahmer was in prison.

Joyce Dahmer said that when she voiced concern for her son's safety in prison, he would say something to the effect of, "It doesn't matter, Mom. I don't care if something happens to me."

He soon would get his wish.

On the morning of November 26, 1994, Dahmer left his cell to go to his work assignment. Two other inmates, Jesse Anderson and Christopher Scarver went with him. The inmates were left unsupervised while they were cleaning the showers and bathroom in the prison gym.

Several minutes later, Scarver bludgeoned Dahmer to death with a metal weightlifting bar as he was cleaning a locker. Scarver also attacked Anderson with the same weapon.

Dahmer and Anderson were rushed to a nearby hospital and both died shortly after they were admitted. Scarver, who was serving a life sentence for a murder he committed in 1990, told prison investigators he did not plan the attack in advance. Anderson was also serving a life sentence for the 1992 murder of his wife, Barbara who he stabbed nine times.

He said that morning that, "God told me to do it. Jesse Anderson and Jeffrey Dahmer are dead." Scarver did tell a prison guard that he had concealed the metal on him prior to the attack.

Scarver said that he was disgusted by Dahmer's crimes and that right before he killed him, Scarver presented a newspaper to Dahmer detailing some of the horrific things he'd done. Scarver demanded to know if what the paper was saying was true.

When Dahmer replied that it was true, Scarver was sent into a rage and killed him. Scarver also alleged that Dahmer was very vocal about his crimes in prison and that he would often say that the human flesh he cooked was better than the prison good.

Allegedly the prison guards were aware of Scarver's hatred of Dahmer and that they had left the two men alone on purpose so that Scarver would kill Dahmer.

He also recalled that Dahmer did not fight back, yell, or make any other noise during the assault and behaved like he didn't care that he was being murdered. Scarver was sentenced to two additional life sentences for the murders of Anderson and Dahmer.

In 2015, Scarver said that the murders of Dahmer and Anderson were the result of an incident were they poked him in the back one day and laughed at him when he turned around to face them. Scarver also said that Dahmer was disliked so much by their fellow inmates that he had to have at least one prison guard with him at all times to prevent being attacked.

Dahmer died at 9:10 a.m on November 28, 1994. Per the request in his will, he was cremated and his ashes were divided between his parents.

The apartment building where the majority of Dahmer's crimes took place, the Oxford Apartments were demolished in November 1992. The site has remained empty for years.

Dahmer's parents and stepmother maintained that they still loved Jefferey despite the horrible crimes he committed. Lionel Dahmer wrote a book called A Father's Story in 1994. He and his wife, Shari both refused to change their surname. David Dahmer on the other hand did change his last name and refused to discuss his brother's crimes.

# Close

There is no doubt that Jeffrey Dahmer committed some of the most gruesome, violent, and horrific murders of all time. Even though Dahmer is put into the same category as similar infamous killers like Ted Bundy and John Wayne Gacy, his slight show of remorse and overall non-threatening personality and lack of outward charm makes Dahmer stand out.

These aspects of his personality and his shy nature counteract the often true stereotype of the charming and manipulative psychopathic serial killer. This makes him even more terrifying. Dahmer's selective victim profile also set him apart from other prominent killers as does his sexuality, but those aspects didn't make him any less terrifying, especially to those in a marginalized population that Dahmer was preying on.

Dahmer's show of remorse for his crimes is another startling aspect of this case that is baffling. In his interviews when he is recalling his crimes, he appears as if he is disgusted with himself for what he'd done, and he was.

Regardless of the court's ruling stating that Dahmer did not suffer from a mental illness of any kind is not accurate at all because an individual would have to be mentally ill.

Had Dahmer been alive in a different time where the things he struggled with: alcohol addiction, his homosexuality, and mental illness were less stigmatized, seventeen young men might still be alive today.

Printed in Great Britain
by Amazon